NATIONAL GEOGRAPHIC

Machines in Health

USING SIMPLE MACHINES

Caroline Snow

PICTURE CREDITS
Cover: teenage girl in a wheelchair, Photodisc; surgeon with
scalpel, Photodisc; doctor checking a boy's throat © Jose Luis
Pelaez, Inc./Corbis/Tranz.

page 1 © Macmillan Publishers New Zealand; page 4 (bottom left),
Corbis; page 4 (bottom right), Photodisc; page 5 (top) © Ed
Bock/Corbis/Tranz; page 5 (bottom left) © Corbis/Tranz; page 5
(bottom right), Corbis; page 7 (left) © James Burke/Time Life
Pictures/Getty Images; page 7 (right), Photodisc; page 8
© Jose Luis Pelaez, Inc/Corbis/Tranz; page 9 © Chris Ladd/Taxi/
Getty Images; page 10, Photodisc; page 11, Brand X Pictures;
page 12 © Richard Olivier/Corbis/Tranz; page 13 © Fotomorgana/
Corbis/Tranz; page 14, Photodisc; page 15 © Walter Hodges/
Corbis/Tranz; page 21 (left), Photodisc; page 21 (middle, right)
© Macmillan Publishers New Zealand; page 29, Corbis.

Illustrations: pages 10–18 by Andrew Aguilar;
pages 23–26 by Pat Kermode.

Produced through the worldwide resources of the National
Geographic Society, John M. Fahey, Jr., President and Chief
Executive Officer; Gilbert M. Grosvenor, Chairman of the Board;
Nina D. Hoffman, Executive Vice President and President, Books
and Education Publishing Group.

PREPARED BY NATIONAL GEOGRAPHIC SCHOOL PUBLISHING
Ericka Markman, Senior Vice President and President, Children's
Books and Education Publishing Group; Steve Mico, Vice President
and Editorial Director; Marianne Hiland, Executive Editor; Richard
Easby, Editorial Manager; Jim Hiscott, Design Manager; Kristin
Hanneman, Illustrations Manager; Matt Wascavage, Manager of
Publishing Services; Sean Philpotts, Production Manager.

EDITORIAL MANAGEMENT
Morrison BookWorks, LLC

PROGRAM CONSULTANTS
Dr. Shirley V. Dickson, Program Director, Literacy, Education
Commission of the States; James A. Shymansky, E. Desmond Lee
Professor of Science Education, University of Missouri-St. Louis.

National Geographic Theme Sets program developed by Macmillan
Education Australia, Pty Limited.

Published by the National Geographic Society
1145 17th Street, N.W.
Washington, D.C. 20036-4688

ISBN: 07922-47574

Printed in Hong Kong.

2011 2010 2009 2008
4 5 6 7 8 9 10 11 12 13 14 15

Contents

Using Simple Machines...................4

Machines in Health.........................6

Think About the Key Concepts...............19

Visual Literacy
Labeled Photograph.........................20

Genre Study
How-to Books...............................22

Wheelchair User Manual....................23

Apply the Key Concepts.....................27

Research and Write
Write Your Own User Manual................28

Glossary....................................31

Index.......................................32

Using Simple Machines

When you hear the word *machine*, what is the first thing that comes to your mind? Perhaps you think of a dishwasher or a vacuum cleaner. These are both machines, but a broom and a knife are also machines. Basically, a machine is any kind of device that helps you do something more easily. People use simple machines every day—at home, in sports, on construction sites, and in health care.

 ## Key Concepts ....

1. Machines use force to help people do work.

2. There are six simple machines.

3. Compound machines use two or more simple machines operating together.

Where Machines Are Found

In the Home

Simple machines help people with many different tasks in the home.

In Sports

Simple machines are a part of many types of sports equipment.

In this book you will learn about simple machines used in health care, such as this tongue depressor.

In Construction

Simple machines make the construction of buildings possible.

In Health

Simple machines are an important part of health care.

Machines
in Health

When did you last visit the hospital, the doctor, or the dentist? If you have been in a hospital, you will have seen some very complicated machines. Some of these machines take x-rays or scans of the inside of your body. Other machines work in place of patients' lungs while they undergo surgery. But did you know that when your doctor or your dentist uses a simple tool such as a needle, he or she is using a machine?

Today, health care workers use many complex machines when they work with their patients. These machines help them provide a level of care that would not have been possible years ago. Think of the machines that help doctors perform surgery. Machines in intensive care units at hospitals can carry out the functions of the human body to keep patients alive. Even with all this technology, however, health care workers still use many simple machines, such as needles, scalpels, tweezers, and tongue depressors.

Machines – Past and Present

The machines we use today are based on some basic or simple machines that were invented thousands of years ago. These earliest machines were made of natural materials and helped people in their daily lives.

For example, archaeologists know that people long ago made needles out of bone to stitch their clothing. Today, doctors use needles to stitch together bad cuts to help them heal. People long ago also invented the **lever** to help them move objects, and the **wedge** to help them cut and split things. Today, doctors use tongue depressors to hold down a patient's tongue. A tongue depressor is a lever. Dentists use drills to remove the decayed parts of teeth. The tip of a drill is a wedge.

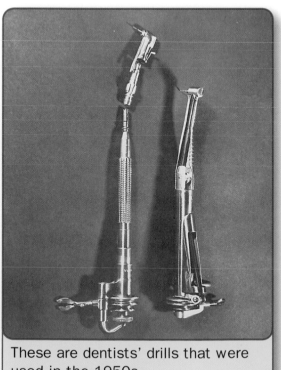

These are dentists' drills that were used in the 1950s.

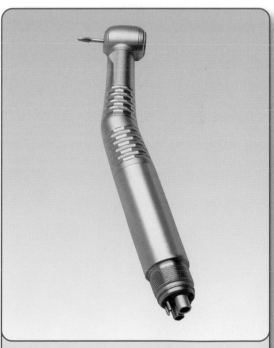

Today, dentists use modern drills, like this one.

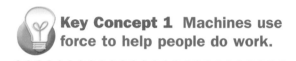

Key Concept 1 Machines use force to help people do work.

Force and Work

To understand how machines operate, you first need to understand **force** and work. Force is something that causes, changes, or stops the movement of an object. When health care workers perform any task, they use force. Force is used to move patients around a hospital. Force is used when a bandage is wrapped around a swollen ankle. Force is applied to cover a cut on someone's knee. The bandage keeps a force pressing down on the cut to stop the flow of blood. A doctor uses force to remove a splinter, set a bone, or even make an incision.

> force
> something that moves, changes, or stops an object

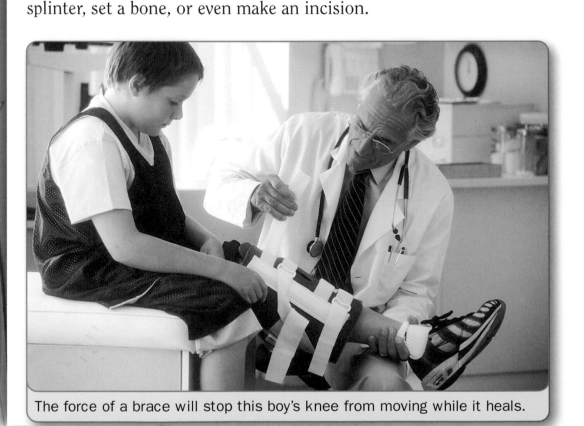

The force of a brace will stop this boy's knee from moving while it heals.

When health care workers use force to move, stop, or change an object, they are doing **work**. In science, the word *work* means the result of force moving, stopping, or changing an object.

When health care workers do an easy job, such as putting an adhesive bandage on a cut, they are doing work. They are stopping the flow of blood from the wound. On the other hand, if they try to move heavy equipment but cannot move it at all, they are not doing work. They might use a great deal of effort, but no work is done.

People use **machines** to make work easier, or to make certain tasks possible. Machines make work easier by giving people a **mechanical advantage**. A mechanical advantage means a person can use a smaller amount of force to get work done.

Machines do not decrease the amount of work that needs to be done. Instead, they change the way the work is done. For example, it requires less force to extract a splinter using tweezers than it does by using fingers alone. This is because tweezers offer a mechanical advantage.

Applying an adhesive bandage is easy, but it is still doing work.

The Six Simple Machines

There are six **simple machines** that make work easier. Simple machines are devices that change how forces act. People invented simple machines thousands of years ago. Over the years, these machines have changed the way people work.

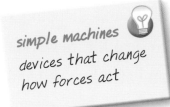

simple machines
devices that change
how forces act

The Wedge A wedge is a simple machine with one or more sloping sides. It often ends in a sharp edge or point. When you force a wedge into an object, it splits the object apart.

Wedges are often used for cutting or piercing. In health care, the blades of scalpels and surgical scissors are cutting wedges. Needles are piercing wedges. The sharper the point or edge of a wedge, the less force is needed to cut or pierce something.

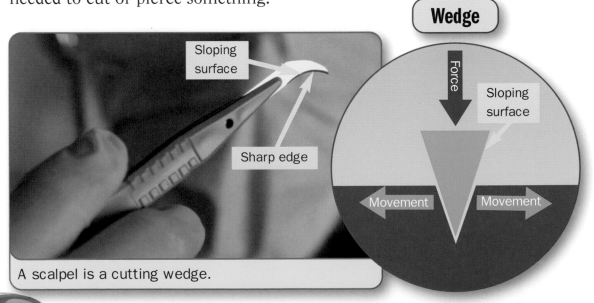

A scalpel is a cutting wedge.

The Lever A lever is a straight rod or bar with three parts. These parts are a load arm, a force arm, and a **fulcrum**. The load arm holds a **load**, while force is applied to the force arm. The fulcrum works as a pivot on which the lever rests. A lever can change the amount of force needed to move something. The mechanical advantage of a lever increases as the fulcrum is moved closer to the load.

There are different ways to use a lever. The force, fulcrum, and load can change places depending on the type of work that needs to be done. A machine such as forceps has two levers. These levers work in the same way as the lever in the first diagram. The fulcrum is between the force and the load.

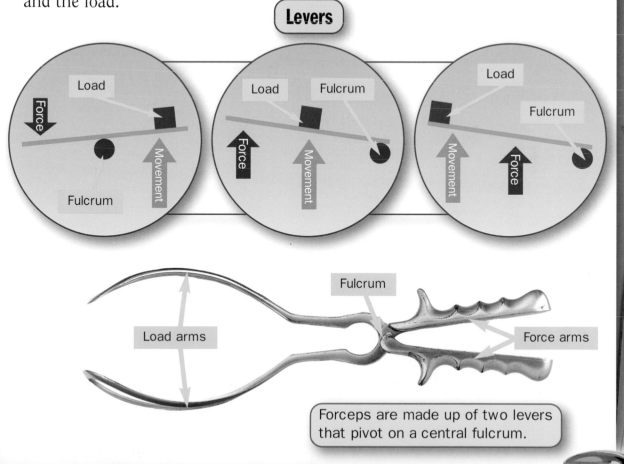

Forceps are made up of two levers that pivot on a central fulcrum.

The Inclined Plane An **inclined plane**, or ramp, is a flat, slanted surface with a low end and a high end. Ramps make it easier to move objects up and down. Instead of lifting an object straight up, you can push or pull the object up the ramp. For example, it is easier to push a wheelchair up a ramp than to lift it up the stairs.

Ramps or inclined planes make work easier by reducing the amount of force needed to move an object up. The less steep the inclined plane is, the easier the job becomes. For example, it is easier to push a wheelchair up a slight but long incline than up a steep but short incline. It would take more force to move an object up the steep ramp in the second diagram than up the less steep ramp in the first diagram.

Inclined Plane

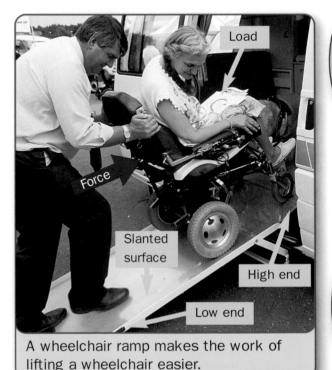

A wheelchair ramp makes the work of lifting a wheelchair easier.

Load

Force

Slanted surface

High end

Low end

High end

Load

Force

Low end

Slanted surface

The Screw A **screw** is a simple machine related to the inclined plane. A screw is an inclined plane that is twisted into a spiral around a pole. The core of a screw is the pole, and the twisted ramp is called the screw's **thread**. The distance between the edges of the thread is called the **pitch**.

When a screw is turned, the thread twists into the object at the tip of the screw, moving the screw in. For each turn, the distance the screw moves into the object equals the pitch. It takes less force but more turns to insert a screw with a smaller pitch. To remove a screw, it must be turned in the opposite direction. It is very difficult to pull a screw straight out, so screws are useful for holding objects tightly together.

Doctors use screws to repair some fractures, or breaks in bones. The broken bone is fixed in position and supported with screws. The screws help the bone heal and become strong enough to bear weight again.

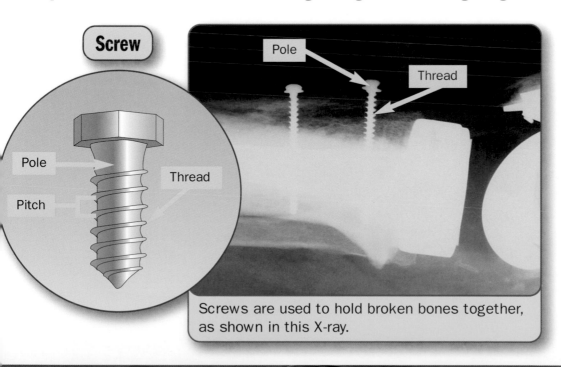

Screw

Pole

Thread

Pole

Thread

Pitch

Screws are used to hold broken bones together, as shown in this X-ray.

The Wheel and Axle For centuries, the **wheel and axle** has helped people move themselves and their belongings from place to place. This machine is made up of a wheel that turns on a pole called an axle. The wheel and axle always turn together. Turning the bigger wheel makes the smaller axle turn more slowly but with more force. Turning the axle makes the wheel turn more quickly but with less force.

This simple machine can be used for more than just moving people and objects. It can also be used to generate a strong turning force. For example, the valve of an oxygen tank consists of a handle—the wheel—attached to an axle that is connected to the opening mechanism inside the tank. People turn the handle a long distance, which turns the axle a shorter distance but with a stronger force. This force opens the tank.

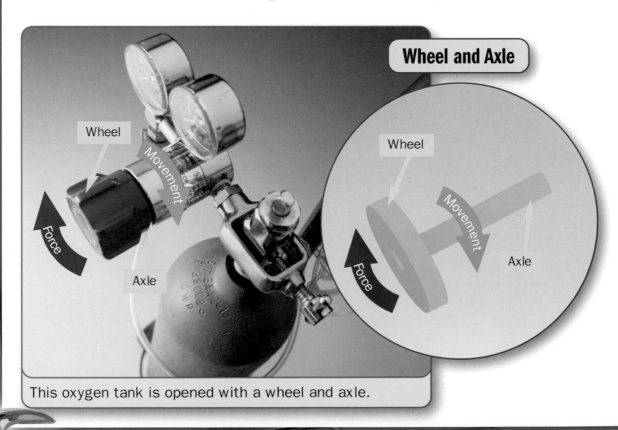

Wheel and Axle

Wheel

Movement

Force

Axle

Wheel

Movement

Force

Axle

This oxygen tank is opened with a wheel and axle.

The Pulley A **pulley** also has a wheel and an axle. But a pulley has a grooved wheel that spins around an axle that does not turn. A rope passing over the wheel is attached to a load. A force applied to the other end of the rope lifts the load. With a single pulley, the amount of force needed to lift the load is equal to the weight of the load. A single pulley simply changes the direction of a force. Pulling down is usually an easier motion than lifting up. Single pulleys are used in health care to elevate broken bones while they are healing.

Some pulleys make work easier by changing the amount of force needed to do the work. Two or more pulleys can be combined in different ways to change the amount of force needed to do work. In such systems, a small force on the rope can be used to move a heavy load. However, the rope must be pulled a long distance to move the load just a short distance.

In health care, pulley systems on exercise machines help patients to strengthen their muscles when they are recovering from injury.

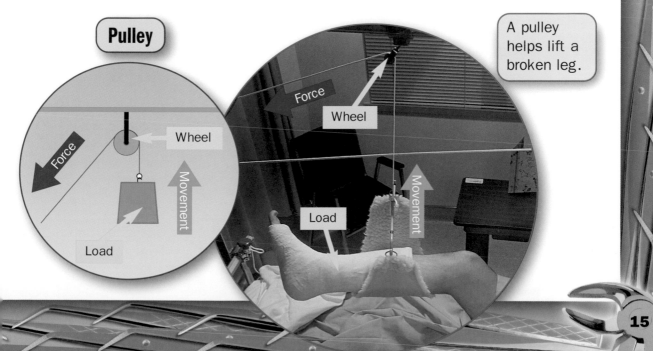

Pulley

Force

Wheel

Movement

Load

A pulley helps lift a broken leg.

Force

Wheel

Movement

Load

Key Concept 3 Compound machines use two or more simple machines operating together.

Working with Machines in Health Care

Health care workers use machines to make work easier. Machines such as wheelchairs allow patients to get around more easily. Surgeons use machines such as scalpels and surgical scissors while performing delicate surgery.

Some machines used in health care are made up of just one simple machine. Some are a combination of two or more simple machines. Machines that are made up of more than one simple machine are called **compound machines**.

> compound machines
>
> machines that are made up of more than one simple machine

Surgical Scissors People in health care use surgical scissors to cut things like thread. A pair of surgical scissors is a compound machine. It consists of two levers that pivot on a central fulcrum. The sharp edge of each lever is a wedge. When people apply force on the force arms, the wedges on the load arms can cut through things.

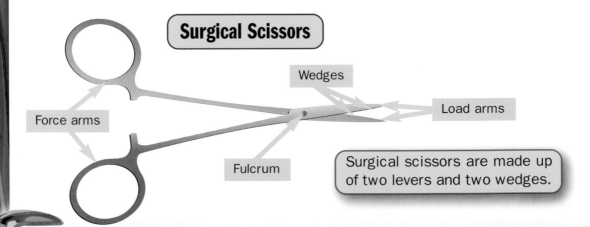

Surgical Scissors

Wedges

Load arms

Force arms

Fulcrum

Surgical scissors are made up of two levers and two wedges.

Prosthetic Arm Sometimes, a person loses an arm in an accident, or has to have it amputated, or removed, because of disease. Doctors can replace the lost arm with a prosthetic, or artificial, one. Just like a natural arm, a prosthetic arm functions as a lever, with the elbow as the fulcrum. Force lifting the top of the forearm raises a load held in the artificial hand. Screws help hold the artificial arm together. In some artificial arms, force is applied to the artificial forearm and hand using a system of pulleys that are connected to the person's healthy shoulder.

Prosthetic Arm

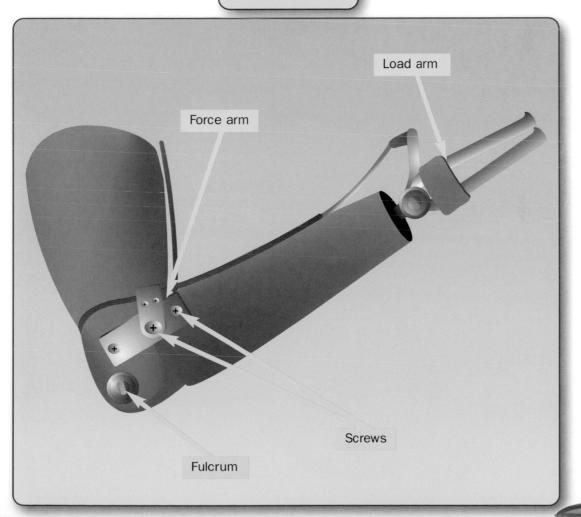

Load arm

Force arm

Screws

Fulcrum

Wheelchair A wheelchair is a compound machine that helps people who are sick or have disabilities move around easily. It uses wheels and axles to do work. The circular handles on the wheels are smaller than the large wheels of the wheelchair. These handles act as the axle of the wheel and axle machine. The person in the wheelchair turns the handles, or axles, forward. This causes the large wheels to turn forward also. The handles and wheels always turn together. Turning the handles with a strong force turns the large wheels more quickly but with less force.

The wheelchair also uses levers to work. Tipping levers at the back of a wheelchair allow it to be lifted up onto a curb. The tipping levers work as force arms, and the back wheels become fulcrums. Pushing down on the levers lifts the front wheels, so the wheelchair can be lifted onto a curb more easily.

Wheelchair

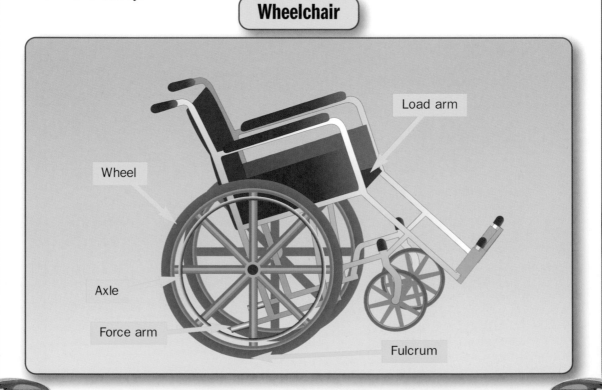

Load arm

Wheel

Axle

Force arm

Fulcrum

Think About the Key Concepts

Think about what you read. Think about the pictures and diagrams. Use these to answer the questions. Share what you think with others.

1. What are three things that force can do to an object? Give an example of each.

2. In science, what is the connection between force and work?

3. Name the six simple machines. Explain how each one can help people work.

4. Give two examples of compound machines. Explain how they help people work.

Labeled Photograph

Photographs show you real-life examples of ideas discussed in books or articles.

A **labeled photograph** provides extra information. The labels show you which important parts of the photograph you should be looking at.

Look back at the labeled photographs on pages 10–15. These are labeled examples of simple machines used in health care. The labeled photograph on page 21 shows three compound machines used by dentists.

How to Read a Labeled Photograph

1. Read the title.
   The title tells you the subject, or what the photograph is about.

2. Read the labels and caption.
   Labels and captions tell you about the subject and its parts.

3. Study the photograph.
   Connect the information in the photograph to what you have read in the text.

Dentists' Instruments

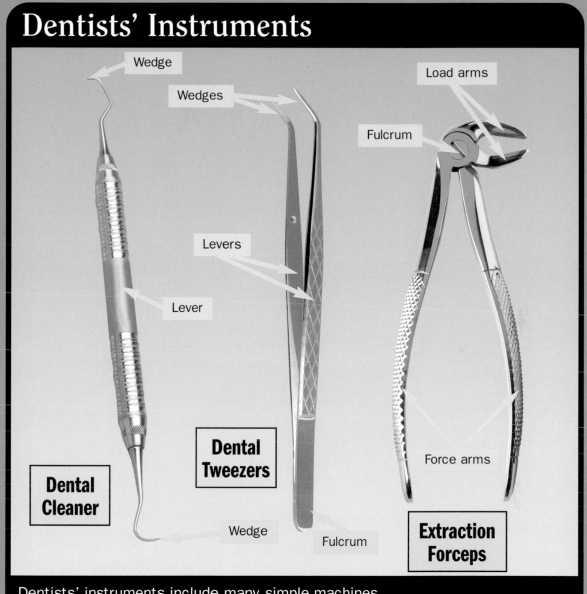

Wedge

Wedges

Load arms

Fulcrum

Levers

Lever

Dental Tweezers

Dental Cleaner

Wedge

Fulcrum

Force arms

Extraction Forceps

Dentists' instruments include many simple machines.

What Can You See?

Read the photograph by following the steps on page 20. Now look back at the diagrams of compound machines on pages 16–18. Can you draw a basic diagram showing the simple machines in dentists' instruments?

How-to Books

The purpose of **how-to books** is to give directions. How-to books take many forms.

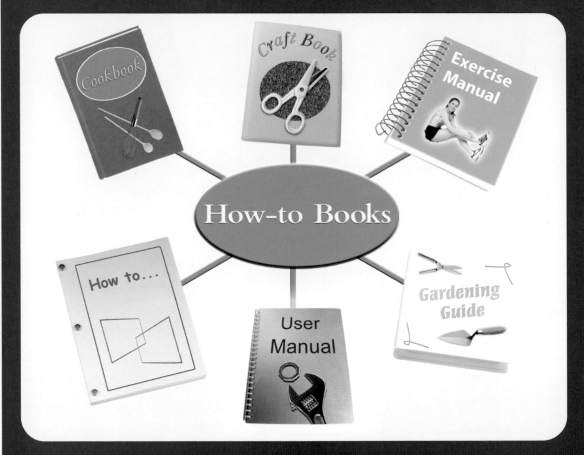

You use different how-to books to find out how to do different things. If you want to know how to use a machine, you read a **user manual**. User manuals come with machines when you buy them.

User manuals give you all the information you need to know before you use a machine. They tell you how to operate the machine. They also tell you how to care for the machine and how to use it safely.

Wheelchair User Manual

Congratulations on buying your new wheelchair. Inside this user manual, you will find directions on using your wheelchair. You will also learn how to clean and care for it. Follow these instructions, and you will get many years of use from your wheelchair.

The **title** tells you which machine the user manual is for.

Parts of the Wheelchair

Subheads break the information into easy-to-find sections.

Labels show the parts of the machine.

1. handles
2. folding backrest
3. armrests
4. armrest frames
5. brake levers
6. brakes
7. footrests
8. front wheels
9. tipping lever
10. hand rims
11. rear wheels

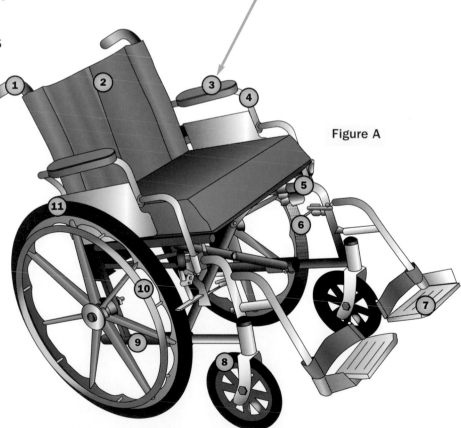

Figure A

Safety Precautions

Wheelchairs can be dangerous if they are not used correctly. Follow these safety precautions to ensure the safety of the wheelchair occupant.

- Try to avoid steep slopes. If you cannot avoid a steep slope, slowly move the wheelchair backward down the slope.
- Always move the wheelchair at a speed you can control.
- Always set the brakes when the wheelchair has stopped moving, even on a flat surface.
- When following another wheelchair, always keep one wheelchair distance apart.
- Watch out for drains, curbs, and other obstacles in your path.
- Keep the wheelchair on sidewalks and walkways. Avoid using the road wherever possible.
- Do not take the wheelchair on an escalator.
- Do not lift the wheelchair by the armrests or wheels.
- Do not tip the wheelchair forward.

Important information is presented in bulleted lists so it is easy to find and read.

Setting up the Wheelchair

Unfolding the Wheelchair

Care must be taken to unfold the wheelchair correctly before use.

- Release the latches below and behind the armrests.
- Push down on both sides of the seat.
- Do not force the chair open.
- Place the cushion on the seat.
- Swivel the footrests into a horizontal position.

Folding the Wheelchair

The wheelchair can be quickly folded for easy storage and transport.

- Take off the seat cushion (Figure B).

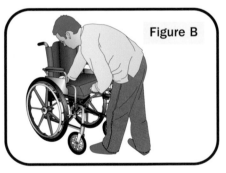

Figure B

- Put the footrests in an upright position.
- Push the handles down and forward to fold the chair.
- Secure the latches below and behind the armrests.

Adjusting the Footrests

The height of the footrests can be adjusted to suit the occupant.

- Press and hold the button on the inside of the front tube to move each footrest up or down (Figure C).

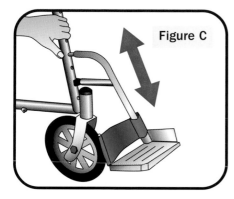

Figure C

- Release the button into the hole at the desired height.
- Set the footrest height so that the wheelchair occupant's thighs are horizontal and at right angles to his or her shins.

Using the Wheelchair: the Occupant

Moving Forward and Backward

- Grip the hand rims on the outside of the rear wheels.
- Push the hand rims forward to move the wheelchair forward.
- Pull the hand rims backward to move the wheelchair backward.

Turning the Wheelchair

- To turn a corner, hold one wheel still while pushing the other wheel forward.
- To turn around in a tight space, pull one wheel backward and push the other wheel forward.

Using the Wheelchair: a Helper

Getting the Wheelchair up Curbs

- Push the wheelchair up to the curb so that the front wheels are almost touching it.
- Push down on the tipping lever with your foot while pushing back and down on the handles to balance the chair on its rear wheels.
- Lower the front wheels to the pavement and push the chair forward.
- Lift the rear wheels onto the pavement.

Getting the Wheelchair down Curbs

- Position the wheelchair so that its back is facing the road and the rear wheels are on the edge of the curb.

- Push down on the tipping lever with your foot. Push back and down on the handles to balance the chair on its rear wheels. Move backward.

- Lower the rear wheels gently onto the road. Make sure they touch the ground at the same time.

Caring for the Wheelchair

Checking the Parts

You should check the parts of the wheelchair regularly to ensure that they are in good working condition.

- At least once a week, check that the brakes are secured tightly and are working well. Apply a little oil on the brake linkage once a year to keep the brakes working smoothly.

- Every week, check that the front wheels rotate easily. The wheels should be able to swivel freely.

- Put a little oil on the moving parts once a year to ensure they move smoothly.

- Check that all the nuts and bolts are tight.

- Take the wheelchair to a service center once a year to be thoroughly inspected and serviced.

Cleaning the Wheelchair

- If the upholstery is dirty or dusty, clean it with a damp cloth. Warm soapy water can be used to remove marks (Figure D).

- Clean the paintwork with a damp cloth. Then dry it with a dry cloth. Apply a car or furniture wax to keep it shiny.

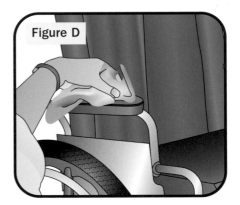

Figure D

Checking the Upholstery

The upholstery needs to be checked every six months for wear.

- Look for any damage, tears, or cuts.

- Check that the screws that hold the upholstery in place are tight and not damaged.

- If you do find damage, take the wheelchair to a service center—it may need to be repaired.

Apply the **Key Concepts**

Key Concept 1 Machines use force to help people do work.

Activity

Think of four ways that people do work in health care. Create a concept web to show the different types of work. For each type of work, write whether the force moves, stops, or changes an object. Label the center of your concept web "Work and Health."

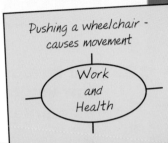

Pushing a wheelchair - causes movement

Work and Health

Key Concept 2 There are six simple machines.

Activity

Think of two examples of simple machines found in health care. Draw these machines. Then label the parts that make them simple machines.

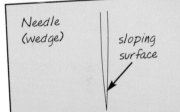

Needle (wedge)

sloping surface

Key Concept 3 Compound machines use two or more simple machines operating together.

Activity

Draw two compound machines found in health care. Then label the different simple machines found within them. One has been started for you on the right.

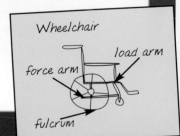

Wheelchair

load arm

force arm

fulcrum

Write Your Own User Manual

You have read the user manual for the wheelchair. Now you can think of a different machine that is used in health care and write a user manual for it.

1. Study the Model

Look back at the user manual on pages 23–26. What information is presented under each section? How do bulleted lists make the information easy to find and read? How do diagrams help you understand the information in the user manual?

2. Choose a Machine

Think of a machine that is used in health care. Draw the design of your machine. Make notes on what job the machine does and how the machine operates. Think of any safety precautions users will need to be told about.

User Manual

◆ Present the information in bulleted lists.

◆ Use diagrams to support the text.

◆ Break the information into easy-to-find sections.

◆ Include important safety precautions.

3. Write a User Manual

Use subheads that are similar to the ones in the wheelchair user manual to write a user manual for your machine. Present the important information clearly in bulleted lists.

4. Draw Diagrams

Draw a diagram and label the different parts of your machine. Label all the parts that you refer to in the text. Then draw smaller diagrams to help illustrate the information in your bulleted lists.

5. Read over Your Work

Read over your user manual, correcting any spelling mistakes or punctuation errors. Make sure your user manual is easy to understand. Are your instructions for use easy to follow? Have you listed all the safety precautions? Did you describe how to care for the machine? Do your diagrams clearly illustrate the text? Is there any other information the user of your machine might need to know?

Safety Precautions

- Only a health care professional should operate the machine.

- It is important to get a professional to service the machine at least once every three months.

Present Your Machine

Now that you have chosen a machine and written a user manual for it, you can present the machine to the rest of the class.

How to Present Your Machine

1. Copy your labeled diagram onto an overhead transparency.
Draw the diagram clearly so you can show the different parts of your machine to the class.

2. Explain your machine to the class.
Take turns presenting your machines. Show the class the different parts of your machine on the overhead projector. Explain to the class what the machine is used for and how the machine works.

3. Explain the safety precautions.
It is important to follow the safety precautions carefully when you use any machine. Tell the class of any possible dangers with using your machine. Explain how to use the machine in the safest way possible.

4. Show the class how to care for the machine.
Tell the class how to clean, store, and care for the parts of your machine to keep it in the best working order.

Glossary

compound machines – machines that are made up of more than one simple machine

force – something that moves, changes, or stops an object

fulcrum – the fixed point on which a lever turns or swivels

inclined plane – a slanted surface that is higher at one end than the other; also called a ramp

lever – a straight bar or rod that rotates about a fixed place

load – an object that a simple machine moves, stops, or changes

machines – tools or other devices that help people do work

mechanical advantage – the extent to which a machine changes force and direction

pitch – the distance between the edges of the thread on a screw

pulley – a grooved wheel and rope system, used to move loads

screw – a pole with a ridge called a thread that spirals around it

simple machines – devices that change how forces act

thread – a sloped ridge that wraps around the pole of a screw

wedge – an object with one or more sloping sides that may end in a sharp edge or point

wheel and axle – a wheel joined to a pole or rod

work – the result of force moving, stopping, or changing an object

Index

compound machine 16, 18

force 8–18

force arm 11, 16–18

fulcrum 11, 16–18

inclined plane 12–13

lever 7, 11, 16–18

load 11–12, 15–18

load arm 11, 16–18

mechanical advantage 9, 11

pivot 11

pulley 15, 17

screw 13, 17

simple machine 4–7, 10, 13–14, 16

thread 13

tool 6, 9

wedge 7, 10, 16

wheel and axle 14, 18

work 6, 8–12, 15–16, 18